MW01107959

*Soul Pathways: Inspirational Messages Channelled from
Spirit Through Australian Mediums* by Marcia Quinton and Ernest M. Henry
Published by Australian eBook Publisher
www.AustralianEbookPublisher.com.au
© Marcia Quinton and Ernest M. Henry

1st Edition 2017, pbk.
ISBN: 978-1-925635-11-9
Publishing services by: Australian eBook Publisher

National Library of Australia Cataloguing-in-Publication entry:
Creator: Quinton, Marcia, author.
Title: Soul Pathways : Inspirational Messages Channelled from Spirit Through
Australian Mediums / Marcia Quinton and Ernest M. Henry

ISBN: 9781925635119 (paperback)
ISBN: 9781925635126 (ebook : epub)
ISBN: 9781925635133 (ebook : kindle)

Subjects: Channeling (Spiritualism)--Australia.
Inspiration. Spiritual direction.

Other Creators/Contributors:
Henry, Ernest M., author.

Also available as an ebook from major ebook vendors.

SOUL
PATHWAYS

INSPIRATIONAL MESSAGES
CHANNELLED FROM SPIRIT
THROUGH AUSTRALIAN MEDIUMS

Australian
eBook
Publisher

MARCIA QUINTON &
ERNEST M. HENRY

Preface

This book is dedicated to Spirit and their work in developing a higher evolving consciousness in the world. We give thanks to Spirit for the continued evolution of humankind and spreading their message of love.

I have the privilege to be working with this group of developing mediums who are embarking upon the path of enlightenment. I have the pleasure of watching each of them grow, and to slowly see them become aware of their own unique gift unfolding. I am privileged to witness the Spirit guiding them and encouraging them to share their words with life.

We are all connected through the soul on our journey through life.

We may not be the same, but as two souls connect, they are drawn toward a common goal and each helps the other. Within a group, many souls are working to advance from this platform in life. We are regarded by Spirit capable of being effective in assisting each other to unfold another part of our earthly garment, as well as seeking and understanding the soul's purpose, and fulfilling a small part of it. We may not touch each other for long but it awakens us, as is needed at this very time in our lives.

Every soul seeking enlightenment which is touched or embraced by Spirit is given a gift to develop and grow with. Within that gift, there is a silent request seeking the seeker to impart the messages to others who come to them in life. There is potential in all to receive some incredible words like a flow of magic from the Spirit World—guides, teachers, healers, mentors, and masters—it's the responsibility of all who are touched to use these words to benefit not only themselves but others as well.

Those who are inspired or channel are given words of "longing from Spirit" to pass on into life, to open a door for others who will then be touched by the magic of love and healing.

Today, you may open a page of this book and see some of the magic that has flowed through these beautiful souls. Each writer has taken the risk of putting their words out there for others to benefit from, and to honor those who have guided them.

For me, as their teacher and guide in life, on a short journey, I am proud that they took the risk, and I am elated for them and for Spirit. The words of my students are beautiful, as I have seen their struggle to let go and give. I have witnessed each writer's decision to develop and I have watched them open their minds to see Spirit with new sight and let go enough for it to happen.

The words that flow are a rich source of unclouded information from another dimension. The words of Spirit seek only to comfort and help humanity. By reading these words, Spirit will help you to move away from shadows on a gloomy day, take time to look after yourself, breathe in fresh air, look around at life with a new insight and enjoy living your life.

Simply sit and allow the soul time to grow and explore your own capabilities.

To the uninitiated this may seem simple, but the words and messages of Spirit are of love.

These words, as I hear them from each student, are like petals scattered across life to touch all.

Special Thanks

To my Guide and Teacher, Red Feather

This book is my tribute to you for the continual love and support you have shown to me, and many others. You have guided me always to assist and help others and to pause when it all becomes too much for me. You have assisted me endlessly in my development, and with the development of others. Your kindness and compassion always overwhelms me as I struggle through life learning from you.

You inspire me with your effortlessness to love. I have learned never to judge, but to keep on encouraging everyone to move forward in the vast sea of life. You have encouraged me to reach out and grasp opportunities, and grow, holding onto the light always. You have allowed my soul, mind and spirit to grow.

The lessons I have learned throughout life are like petals falling onto the ground as I move forward. Thanks to you, Red Feather, I remember them as they were—positive or negative—but only as lessons not as burdens. Time is an illusion. We have little in life—no time to waste. There will be time enough when we return to the spirit world. So I wish to pause and thank you for a lifetime of love, guidance and a unique friendship, and for all the love you brought into my life through this spiritual foundation.

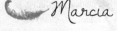

A Very Special Thanks to Ernest M. Henry

Ernest, you are a beacon of light and you constantly shine your light through life giving and supporting those who need it selflessly. You have been an amazing support, and you were instrumental in bringing this book together. It would not have been completed without your constant effort with all of us to complete the work to bring Spirit's words to life in the pages of this unfolding book.

It's been an opportunity for all, but you have given so much more with your enthusiasm and love for this to come to life. You are a gifted spiritual healer, empath, intuitive psychic clairvoyant, and trance medium channeler who channels so many inspiring words from your spirit guides.

Ernest, with your vast knowledge and experience in the many different spiritual modalities and exploration of other religions and cultures, you have so much to offer to so many in life. They will be blessed by your help, teachings and support, as they self-align to their journey and soul purpose. You have a transpersonal gift of knowing when to give and when to pause and listen.

Your heart guides you always, and now it seems as if the Spirit calling is strong for you to open your mind and heart, and walk the spiritual path. You share your heart completely and are always putting every soul first in life.

You, my dear friend, have touched my life and I am blessed to call you a friend.

We all thank you so much for the love you share.

Table of Contents

Introduction

MARCIA QUINTON:

My aim with this book is to bring awareness to others of the wonderful spiritual messages that Spirit brings through each channel. I only have a small group to achieve this with as it allows each student more time. Spirit guides are forever encouraging and inspiring us — they are aware of our world and of our many difficulties. Spirit is aware of what we, as a global community, are dealing with each day, and it tries to enable us to assist others in some small way.

Channelling is where the spirit guides work through the mind. The channel may be fully conscious of a stream of thought from another personality flowing through to them. The blending of the two minds creates a flow of inspirational conversation. It's important to create harmony and balance to allow this connection to work. Spirit impresses and inspires us, allowing its words and thoughts to influence us, and for us to let our minds step aside and let the magic flow. It's important to recognise the difference in communication to that of your own. I am passionate about the power of Spirit and the powerful influence it can bring into our lives to help us serve ourselves and others.

I began my spiritual quest in 1972, following the death of my beloved daughter, Traci. Through my heartache, I felt strong urges to search for answers and look for my daughter. All this was intuitive and in dreams, I was not able to believe that I would never hear from her again.

Throughout my life, since childhood, I had experienced many strange spiritual murmurings. I felt that there was more out there to find. I had a job in a hospital at the time and was working with Irene, a wonderful woman from England who talked to me about her mother being a spiritualist. In time, she explained in detail what all this meant. She encouraged me to seek a Spiritualist Church for help as they could provide me with answers about my daughter.

In my search, the only church of that nature I was able to find was the Enmore Spiritualist Church, so there began my journey. I still remember the feeling that came over me as I walked into the church. I felt I had at long last come home. It shook me as I knew nothing of spiritualist beliefs or practices. The church was located in an old house with old theatre chairs. It was nothing flash or fancy, but everyone was friendly and the vibration was amazing. All this was so new and slightly overwhelming, as I was still so raw from the loss of Traci.

I joined a very large open circle run by the wonderful Ivan Charles, and began my spiritual development. It was a long journey, but I never wavered on the path. Unknown to me, Spirit had plans for my journey. It was an interesting time and many experiences later I was to run the church and assist many others in developing on their own spiritual path.

The introduction of trance mediumship came to me through the circle and it was apparent that this was not understood by all in a large group and it was not Ivan's forte to work with. A small circle was formed with the help of Valerie, who was a medium who appeared in the church at that time, guided by Spirit. It was in this group that I connected with my guide, Red Feather, who I still work with today. Red Feather and I have formed a strong spiritual bond, each achieving the goals we were meant to achieve on this life journey.

I began teaching at Enmore, running many development classes and trance classes. I also took workshops and ran a healing group weekly for two years. After 34 years, I made the change and became a professional working medium and took some time for me. Now I work as a clairvoyant medium and a trance medium/channeller. I am an innovative teacher facilitating classes and workshops. I am a healer, a Reiki master, a rescue medium, a trained counsellor and a spiritual counsellor. I have tremendous love for the work that I do and I respect the Spirit guides I work with who do try hard to assist us.

My goals are simple—to help others in the way Spirit guides me, connecting with spirit guides to share their love and messages with people. However they guide me, I will try to fulfill that journey, knowing that I am human and still fall short in many areas.

ERNEST M. HENRY:

Marcia Quinton's openness, patience and willingness to encourage each person's gift in their own timing, inspires me, as it does others. She shares all her decades of experience and knowledge—with selfless love—with many individuals and groups of people, showing me and others the true meaning of service and trust to others.

The channelled messages from Spirit are quite profound—there is something for every soul in each one of these messages. Read and feel the words with your heart; this will allow you to open up to the messages it has for you.

Meeting Marcia Quinton years ago, brought me back to the present and gave me back balance. She has a gentle approach to teaching her students, many of which are experienced spiritual healers, mediums, psychics and clairvoyants. Marcia has helped us all to bring gifts forward that have lain dormant for various reasons. Each person's journey is so unique. Bit by bit, like a stroke from a feather, Marcia finds a way to break us all down, assisting each one of us to open up our soul's doors and let Spirit come through. She is a teacher's teacher, a clairvoyant, a trance medium, a healer and a humble soul of the highest order.

We honour your journey, dear reader, with love and hope. May you find your soul's purpose and may these words shine a little more light on the path you currently walk on.

STUDENTS:

Marcia is a unique teacher responding to Spirit guidance well. She is forever changing the lessons to suit each student's needs. She listens to their guides and teachers as it is important that each student learns to work with their own Spirit guides and teachers. Marcia has a unique bond with many spirits who guide her to gain the most insightful lessons for all of her students. Every student is different and responds differently, with their individual personalities, which can influence them positively or negatively.

Marcia Quinton

Marcia is a gifted medium and has worked publicly with her gift for over 40 years, demonstrating her ability to give accurate evidence of survival and messages of help and support. Marcia believes that not only does Spirit provide evidence of its existence but it brings love, and provides encouragement, advice, help and support during situations in their loved one's lives here on earth.

She is a very gifted trance medium/channeler and many have been astounded by her brilliance and the phenomena she produces. Marcia is a highly gifted teacher who teaches meditation, helps students open their minds to the psychic/spiritual connection, mediumship classes, trance/channelling classes and inspirational writing. Marcia is an enthusiastic teacher wanting each student to grow to their full potential.

She holds a variety of workshops. Marcia is also a rescue medium and has performed many house cleansings and blessings, shifting negative energies and unwanted guests.

Marcia also works as a hypnotherapist and as a regression therapist.

Marcia is a Reiki master and spiritual healer and had a very successful healing group for two years working with a spirit doctor, Dr Grey.

She enjoys performing ceremonies, house blessings, marriage and relationship blessings, children's spiritual naming days and blessings and spiritual blessings for those needing an uplift in energies. She has demonstrated in many of the spiritualist churches, RSL clubs, psychic fairs and has been a guest on Australian radio stations, including Barry Eaton's "Out There Program" and Captain Pat on C 91.3. Marcia's background in nursing for the past 40 years has been thoroughly enjoyable and has enabled her to use her healing gift for many. Her heart is with those who are in need, and she has willingly given her time to assist in any way she can.

Website: www.Marcia.net.au

Seeker

I sit so still

As I quietly, listen to the soft whispering of my inner light

Consciously I am aware that my soul is gently stirring

With every beat of my heart and every breath I take

Filling me with radiant light, the essence of who I am

With the pure and radiant love pouring forth from my heart

My soul and I gently merge into one

A Moment of Despair

In the silence I hear the whispers of my soul

Drawing me from the shroud of darkness surrounding me

I feel the flow of light the dawning of awareness

Of my heart, my soul, shining through

I pause in thought knowing that I WILL

Make it through this long lonely night

I will embrace the dawn as the darkness fades away

Suffering

Grasping am I

So filled with despair

Wanting, reaching toward the light to

Remove the fear that I feel

To ease away the shadows of doubt

Entangling my thoughts,

I try to lift my mind, my heart and soul

Upward toward a higher light

I ache so deeply within, the pain is unbearable

I cannot wait

I need this light to touch me now

To take away this pain

That fills my heart

Where is my SOUL

My friend and saviour

To help me bear the weight of this suffering

Alone in my confusion I cry

Then I feel the warmth flooding through me

I sleep at last

Free of pain,

My soul has bought me comfort again

Let My Soul Soar

Come fly with me

Let my heart, my soul mingle with yours

Awakening a path of light

As we soar upward

Touching the heart and soul of all eternity

Flowering of the Soul

Pause a moment and let your thoughts alight as the
butterfly gently touches the petals of a flower,
letting itself open to the experience of enjoying the
essence of the flower's radiant beauty.

How aware are you of this wonderful energy that fills
you "every living moment of your life"?

Pause a moment and listen carefully to the stirring,
like the fluttering of wings within.

This is the awakening of the soul responding to you and
your needs and it's ready to fly with you

Our Soul Has a Purpose

A reason

For the journey

Life's quest is to find it

Fulfil it and live it

Seek and you shall find

Your connection with your soul

Music of the Soul

As the dawn breaks

When all is quiet within the world

You hear the stillness, feel the quietness all around

If you stay still and listen

It's when you can hear the music of your soul

Touching the heavenly spheres

In moments of quiet contemplation, meditation

And Prayer or simply reaching for your inner light
you will find sanctuary and silence

There you are touching your soul—you are as one

Soul Leaving

I stand alone along the shore of life

My gaze gently drifting, fading into the distance

My senses are aware of all who are around me

I feel their thoughts and hear their whispers

As they try to assist me, my attention drifts,
their words become muffled

As I hear not them but the silence surrounding me

I see not them—only the light as it draws near

I feel their pain, yet I feel only touched by love

I shift my thoughts further toward that glow

I feel the strings of life pull me, restraining me,
holding me back

I hear the whispers and the weeping and
I struggle to relieve this

But the glow is stronger I feel the love flowing over me

I move toward it, I feel the strings of life
snapping all around me

I am drifting, feeling unsure

I hear voices and yet I feel a sense of freedom

I shift, and move with only my thoughts

I have no pain!

I am drawn toward a light and I glide effortlessly toward it

Then I am consumed with this light

The love—the joy—I feel overwhelms me

My heart and my soul, weep with relief

I am home

Release My Soul

So I may wander freely

Seeking my path following my journey

The flame within

Lights the path

For the soul to guide you

Beginning the Journey

As I unknowingly transverse along the path of life

Fulfilling my life's journey, taking the directions
flowing around me

I am caught unaware

That in a breathtaking moment all is changed

I feel the stirring of my mind longing for that change

I begin each day seeking and searching for
what I do not know

Nor do I understand this intense feeling

But the energy and power within and around pulls
at me all the time

So I begin a journey into the unknown

29

I open myself to meditation

I need to view my life, my path, my journey

Slowly my consciousness begins to awaken,
my thoughts begin to change

I am aware of light, light forms appearing

I am aware of my own heart beat and vibration

Aware of my breath and the of the very core of my being

My thoughts are so crystal clear

I feel the pulse of life deeply all around me so
much more clearly

Within, I feel the beat of my heart reminding me of life

And beating in rhythm with all around me

In my growing awareness I begin to reach deep

I long to touch this unknown part of me

To explore and know what it is that is stirring
beyond my reach

I feel the power from this inner source
moving silently within

It is a blur of light, an awareness that merges into my mind

Surrounding me, its total silence is overwhelming yet
it speaks to every part of me

The flood of light awakens within me a pulse of energy so
pure and so shatteringly beautiful

I am unable to breathe or move with its pureness, its power
and its simple patience with me

I stand frozen in time, unable to move

In that moment of hesitation I feel whole, as if a part of me
has surfaced and completed me

In this powerful moment I am one, then it's gone

I stand still in sheer wonder and amazement

Grasping to comprehend this startlingly amazing revelation

I have felt the core of my being, held it within my grasp

I have seen who I am!

Who I strive to be!

My soul rose like a misty light before me, surrounding,
then consuming, me

For a moment I shed my outer garment

I was a blaze of light

I was in awe of this pure, radiant light—
the beauty of it filled me

I am in awe in the presence of my SOUL

So amazing is this transparent light it shatters all
concepts I ever had

Knowing that My Soul and I are one

A powerful force that guides me from within

I am not alone.

Power

Power is to control

It shifts the balance

It can change the route of life

To feel and experience power emerging is a
wonderful creation

Utilized in the correct way it is phenomenal

Time to awaken the power within

To feel it's ebb and flow like the tides of the sea as it moves
back and forth within the ocean

Cosmic Power from the cosmic ocean is abundant with
energy, untapped, unused for the benefit of all life forms
The stillness and quietness in which it moves is amazing
and it's seen in graceful streams of light as it vibrates within
and around us at all times.

Its powerful loving essence creates amazing changes
around us, as we move in its vastness, a flood of power and
light. We are light, we are energy, we are a unique part of
this energy but we are matter and visible

Another source of power, from our own creation through
the universal energy as we glow with light from the time
we are born as we are gestated within a living human
cell creating us as a solid matter of energy and it allows us
to be able to experience a life as a solid form and yet
we are still energy.

This life form helps us create other matters into solid objects using our own innate ability we brought through in our energy rhythms and patterns. As time passes and our physical energy dissipates through life, our energy fields of the human form can weaken, changing the structure within, and causing us to stop and listen to what is occurring to us within.

A spiritual essence is always present, a guiding light—the Soul—that whispers to us to fulfil our destiny, our journey. We live as energy, as solid forms on earth. When we depart, we are only energy returning to the nucleus of our creator in the vastness of the universe. All of our thoughts are footprints left behind for others to remember, see and use—the path we have trodden upon the planet earth.

All thoughts are matter within, an energy field vibrating around us all. Nothing is unattainable within the living vibrational energy field and we radiate that energy all around us, creating a myriad of emotions that we, in time, allow the Soul to reach out and grasp. We grasp the knowledge and absorb it. Upon the return of our light into the vastness of the universe, it will be filtered through our energies as living information charged with knowledge. Powerful growth occurs as it moves us ever forward into the realms of light.

Releasing the Storm Within

As the wind blew across the ocean, the storm clouds
gathered thick—dark, threatening and creating an
eerie light across the beach.

The wind grew strong, whipping up the waves on the
ocean, creating a thunderous roar—a gigantic sound
booming across the beach louder and louder. I stood
alone, embracing the sound, rejoicing in the wind whipping
through my hair, tugging at me in all directions. I stood
firm, my feet planted within the sand. Alone I might be,
but afraid I was not.

The rain fell lightly at first, creating a beautiful haze.
The mist across the roaring ocean was a restful sight.

The cadence of the rain increased until it was pelting the ground and ocean in a great thunderous roar. The sound rose like a crescendo from earth to heaven, the lightning streaked out across the sky, lighting it up for seconds—beautiful, breathtaking.

The waves tossed themselves around, dancing and embracing that spellbinding light. The storm grew stronger and still I stood as it rode its mighty power all around me like a challenge.

I felt the pain, the anguish, the gripping emotional sadness from deep within. It burst from me in a high pitched wail like the screeching of the relentless wind as it roared across the ocean.

I fell to my knees and let the grief release from me, tears poured from my heart, my mind, my soul—washing into the ocean, taking my pain with them.

My pain lifted slowly from me, with the help of the wind, the rain, the ocean. Spirit carried it away as I released my inner storm.

I stood alone on the shore, uncertain. At that present moment I felt weak and drained but was comforted in knowing that my inner strength would eventually pull me through.

Alone was I, but unafraid of the dawn that had come upon me.

I was calm and felt renewed power flowing through me.

I turned my head toward life, breathing deeply and taking in the freedom that lay ahead of me.

Looking up, I paused as I saw a bird moving outward over the ocean. As I watched the bird, I realised I had released my grief, my loss, and that it had left me free. The further the bird soared, the freer I felt.

My Soul was lighter and able to fly.

Dimly Lit Room

There are shadows dancing off the walls in this dimly lit
room. It's night and all is quiet

The soul sleeps, all is peaceful and quiet

But the magic is happening—the room is filled with light

Spiritual light, as the soul is on a journey

The man sleeping has heard of some sadness, a loved one
touched by illness and is in great difficulty

As his eyes close, his love for that soul draws him across the
divide in time

As he leaves his slumbering body, he soars toward
the call to see if he can lighten the load for those
around the sick soul.

His hands reach out to touch them, allowing his
love to flow to them.

As he moves around the sick bed, he sees the soul leave
and come toward him and he feels his touch and is filled
with emotion. Needing to hold that spirit in his arms a
moment as he knows it's his time to leave. This father of his
is no longer here in life, so he takes his hand and together
they walk toward this amazing light and they remember old
times, fun times, their lives they have shared.

He watches him leave as his dad pauses and looks back at
those around him. He smiles, as it will be another time and
place that they will all meet again.

The man returns to the room and touches the body of his
dad and wishes he was there to comfort those left behind,
but tomorrow he will journey across the ocean to bid his
father a final farewell in life.

He awakens feeling sad but filled with the love of his father.
He knows, as the phone keeps ringing, he has gone.

In his memory is a lily, a gift from his dad, a memory.

Resting in peace, son. I love you.

You are but a Rose in My Heart

You are the rose within my heart that shall always bloom in the love that I feel for you—it shall last forever.

You gave me so much joy and happiness that it tugs at my memories right now, spilling over into words that flow onto this page. They are not enough to express the love I feel or the moments I had with you, or the radiance of your beautiful soul that ever so briefly touched my life and my heart with such joy.

You, my sweetheart, left way too early, long before your time, and I was not ready for your departure. You left ever so abruptly. One moment I held you, loved you, touched you and then, in a whisper of the word "Mum", you were gone forever from my life, leaving such a vibrant living memory in every other way.

It tore my heart in two, and still, to this day,
it's fragile with just the thought of you.

I buried my heart the day I buried you, and for a long time
life was empty and cold, as your sweet smiling face no
longer looked up at me with love and such trust. I know I
never failed you as I could not have loved you more, but
your memory lingers in my life and my heart like the sweet
perfume of the rose, and will forever.

The power of love, how it can hold your life still, and yet
hold your heart powerlessly in its hand, in beauty,
for eternity. You were loved then and you are
loved now and always.

The Soul

It's the power that lies deep within us all

It's the spiritual blueprint of our lives

It's the journey that awakens when the soul enters life

It's the power of who you are and who you will become

In the garden of the soul there are many seeds waiting to germinate and grow within your life

It's the planting that takes the time, to sow a seed into your thoughts

This is the beginning of growth, and rare events begin to take place—a new idea, a journey, a treasure unfolding a beautiful sight to behold right there in front of you

Just pause and let it take root so it will take hold and grow

Nurture it and give it some nourishment at times
so it will grow in fertile soil

It's immeasurable how long it will take

You are in control of your soul and you need to protect it
from outside influences, as they can turn the tide and take
you off course, leaving you stranded.

Once somebody unworthy of your soul has gained what
they want, they will move on

Incidents like this weaken the soul, and you might lose the
confidence to move forward

It may take time to regain the strength to open
the door once more

The path is not always clear, often clouded and misty,
but it will be there

You need to trust and follow as it's too precious to miss

It's powerful to open and join with that energy of the heart.
It also makes you a little more connected to the path of the
soul as you allow love to come forward in your life
as a blessing and a beauty

Take your time, as each journey awakens within you, as
you have time, as it has all been planned and you need to
allow it to merge into your life as a magical opportunity.

The Growth of the Soul

Ernest M. Henry

Born in Fiji, my spiritual journey started as a young boy.
The calming seas and beaches that surrounded me were
my playground, the sounds of palm trees swaying in the
background was the music I listened to, the gentleness
of the people and various island cultures nurtured me,
and gave me an insight to who I was. I had a strong
pull to nature and Spirit. I heard its sounds and voices,
saw its many images, physically and psychically. I felt it
emotionally, every vibration felt in the core of my being,
I was awakened to Spirit early in my childhood. I asked
many questions, but the answers given by many didn't
seem to fulfill my soul's longing or curiosity,
so began my search.

With a paramedical and nursing background spanning over
decades, where everything is based on science and data, I
struggled to reconcile the unending essence of spirituality

with scientific recordable fact. I was fortunate to be involved in many new pioneering medical and surgical technologies, with a long career in the corporate world running many international companies. I have spent decades searching, questioning all that I saw and knew, travelling the world, learning, doing a multitude of courses, building a knowledge base that seemed to never end.

This was my lot, as they say, so Spirit said, "You want proof? This is the hard way around, but go for it." I experienced, saw and learned a lot from many amazing people. I recall the highs and lows while looking for answers, finding out what was real for me, eventually learning the hard way that some things are meant to be seen and felt inwardly, not on some paper. Most of the time the proof is staring us in the face and we can't see or feel it, as we don't trust our intuition, or our own gifts which each of us are given.

Over 30 years, I have worked a lot with energy and healing, utilising various holistic massage therapies. I am a Reiki master and practitioner, an empath and an intuitive. I am one of the early practitioners of Aura Soma, along with other gifted people in this early group.

We are many things on our journey, Christianity, Hindu and Buddhist teachings have been an influence, along with Ernest Holmes' Science of Mind, being one of their first early students. Various meditation techniques have been learnt and used to calm the soul, to travel within to find one's own inner compass to help find your path to your self-truth whatever that is for you. These philosophies have given me a balance and inner richness that I am truly grateful for.

I serve as a spiritual alignment coach, a counsellor, intuitive empath, author, trance channel medium and Reiki master, helping you align you to your self and your truth. I serve all souls as a walking compass, guiding and supporting you when needed, to help you find your path of inner self-alignment towards your own self journey within. My other passions and work are in twin flame and soul journey, inspirational and channelled writings, crystal energies, sacred geometry, sound and light frequencies and science of numbers. These practices make up who I am. .

In sessions, Spirit tends to draw me to past life imagery, answers for you to consider now, or it shows me current situations to address. Whatever message Spirit shows me, I present to you. I have learnt that what we expect to hear, and think we need, is always different to what messages Spirit gives us through any medium, so that trust word comes up for all of us. It's always your choice, your timing, your free will, and what you want to accept as your truth.

Each soul journey is so personal and unique. Through my eventual intent, I surrendered and let go. Judgment of myself and others dropped away like the autumn leaves from a tree, self-change occurred, my self-love increased, my glass was being filled up by Spirit. I was able to face my inner demons in my darkest hours, finding the light switch, turning on the light, leaving the basement of self-doubt. I had found self, my soul, a humility and a strong intuitive pull to Spirit occurred. Through this process, I felt and understood what divine love meant, and what my soul purpose was. My heart reached out to those of like mind—healing, helping souls find their pathway to self—the image like a pebble thrown into a still lake, the rippling effect of the gentle waves extending to all, and beyond the surface. .

For me now the simplest things are our greatest teachers, with Spirit's greatest natural gift a sunrise or sunset, available to all. To share with another soul is a blessing. In that moment of visual and emotional beauty, our soul quietens, we become inner aligned. A stillness occurs, felt by the individual, our soul mate, or twin flame. Herein lies Source—

you, me, all are one again. All the answers you seek are in here. Your self, your divine gift of love awaits, it is now time for you to leave the nest. Fly, surrender and let go, as much awaits you.

I love the quietness of the mountains and the heartbeat of the sea. Any spare time I have is spent getting there. My travels, knowledge, courses and the experiences I have gained have brought me back to my self—the journey that started out as that little boy on the sands of Fiji, who was shown and given so much. I now understand my journey was all about reconnecting to Source—to my self-love—and I will always be grateful to Spirit, and all those very special souls that helped shape me to discover who I am today.

Website: www.ernestmhenry.com

My inner and outer crystal compass: Celestite, Herkimer Diamond, Aquamarine

The Journey of Two Souls

In the beginning we were one

Energy, light, part of a collective consciousnes
all merged together

The time came for each soul to descend to human form

Me in one life, you in another, no memories came
with this life

Just an inner knowing to find each other and
reconnect as one

Two souls, one heart, two journeys, departing
at different times

At a given point we would meet again and be guided back
to Source and each other

Centuries went by, and as the cosmic clock ticked over,
Spirit called. It was time to come together.

It was time to work together as one again. But how would
we know? Then one day a chance meeting, a momentary
glance, for all souls and twin flames are given this chance
of reconnection.

Two souls in recognition of who and what they once were

Two souls now burned brightly as twin flames, both on
their individual journey, and apart

A door had opened. We had both walked through, as do all
twin souls, not knowing what lies ahead

For this is the karmic magic of the journey, glimpses of our
beginning emerged, and the pull of each soul

Was felt, like earth's strong magnetic pull. The connection
was re-established

We each stood before the council of five, brilliant coloured
lights emerging from them, a love felt from them like no
other. We were shown the many lives we had and work we
had done and still needed to do. It's not your time yet to
come home. The keeper of records asked, "Will you fulfil
your karmic destiny and assigned missions?"

We intuitively answered, "Yes" in unison. In a moment we
were allowed to see all the universe in its glory from its
beginning, a kaleidoscope of stars and planets, a collection
of consciousness of all souls. A deep sense of inner peace
enveloped us—we were floating above the ground,
transparent with sparkles of light.

Before me stood one of the five, the brightest of lights, all in transparent white, emanating out immense love. I heard a voice within my whole body. "All souls are of divine love. That is who you are. All souls eventually find themselves through the actions of their heart, and selfless service to others. Go tell all, for everything that needs to be achieved is through this space, so close your eyes our brothers and sisters of light and travel with me to your heart. I am always here in your heart space. Emanate your divine love from here always to the outer world.

We closed our eyes and through our hearts we merged with Source and many souls. At this point we were pure light, immersed totally in an indescribable love never felt before. "This is your home. This is where you come from."

"Go back and teach from your heart. Be not afraid, for there are many in pain who have lost their way and self-love within. We will always guide those who are open and ready with purposeful intent, for their hearts must be open to surrendering and letting go in order for them to find their own door of self-realisation.

"The forefront of their journey within starts with this step. Help them to find their way and open them up by being of service to all that come your way, for this is the journey of each soul and purpose of the twin flame in service to others, yourself, spirit and each other."

Journey of Each Soul

There is no journey without some sacrifice of self

Be thankful for the little things that life gives, feel blessed
for all that you are

And all that you will become

Stop, breathe, listen, for there is great beauty within

And here rests the source of your being

The Calling of the Soul

I feel the pull of energy within me, from the
calling of each soul

I hear the sounds of each voice within

It is not words as we would normally hear it,

But a sound vibration, images flood my mind, for
all are watching

I sit in a large room all in white, no words
need to be spoken

Our hearts, thoughts, are joined as one, all linked together,
love in its purest form is felt and radiated by all

Many lights I see come forth like a rainbow of colours
emanating out of everyone standing there

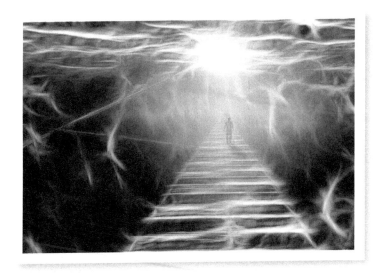

Surrendering to My Soul

Through inner self-acceptance of who you are, you let go

Your heart opens and guides you to your highest good

At that point, you become your own inner compass on
your path of self-truth

Surrender is the language of the heart and is
felt within one's heart

Dear ones, through this one touches their soul and spirit,
and becomes one with Source

The inner vibration, and the change within, gives much-
needed light to others,

As it touches their soul and allows more light into their lives

Let My Soul Soar

Each soul sits in its own karmic capsule

The door between flight and motionless lies within
you as you are your own pilot

It is the individual soul that chooses to self-imprison
through fear or self-judgement

Let go and soar the heights where you are destined to go

Dear ones, remember you are your own
navigator, pilot, plane.

Lift off and see what your view is from above

At present you see only from a ground perspective

Climb to the top of any tree, even as little as two metres
from the ground, and you will see a different outlook

Your soul waits to ascend, and is not concerned with a
destination point, but only that you are willing to take off
and leave the safety of your shoreline, for in that present
moment all your gifts will open up to you
within that journey.

Stand in the Presence of Your Soul

It is only through surrender and self-acceptance that one can stand in the presence of one's soul.

Nothing else matters, for your answers do lie within. It's always been there, behind the door of self-doubt that imprisons us all in fear.

Dear ones, take one inner step forward, for in that present moment of reflection we connect to the essence of our soul and Source.

It is only through surrender to our self, and service to others, that we can find and align to our soul's purpose.

So stand in the present moment of your soul, for all your answers await.

Always see joy in others and have gratitude to all that comes your way, for the greatest gifts lie hidden in the smallest of things.

Listen to My Soul

My soul sings to the beat of my heart

It is the sound of the soul that can be heard by all that listen

Spirit blesses us constantly, it asks us to listen to our soul,

By seeing the beauty in all things, for there is an angelic sound heard by many,

A personal calling, a deep connection with Source.

An energy flow exists, a choir of sound

Can you hear it, moving like a gentle stream?

A synchronicity of events for all on the path

Spirit asks that you let go and put both feet in the water

Listen, feel the sensation of your soul with your eyes and ears as the vibration within your body increases

And sets your soul free, for in that moment of recognition you are one with the sounds of your soul and

The beat of your heart

The Soul's Calling to Each Sunrise and Sunset

From a deep sleep, I awaken daily to the sounds of each sunrise and sunset. It calls me to revisit the kaleidoscope of colours that Source presents daily before me, and for those that will take time to see and touch its beauty.

The beauty of each sunrise and sunset allows me, at that moment, to remember who I am. There is no separation from Source, or anyone, just oneness with all. A glimpse of what collective consciousness of the heart and divine love feels like.

The deep golden orange and subtle blue hues, that present in the sky before me, resonate deeply and speak to my soul, for this is the language of the heart. It's like I have returned home after many lifetimes. At that moment of surrender, a profound stillness envelops me, angelic sounds guide and emanate so softly around me. It lifts me up and fills my soul. My body feels like light. It is a sound that is felt in the heart of all souls and goes out to all who care to listen.

The love and humility I feel brings me to tears, a blessing given in nature's purest form, for all those that will take time to hear their own voices and calling. A gentle reminder that it is never too late to find your path, and start your own inner journey with your own sunrise or sunset.

In the Light of the Soul

Dear ones, your light shines ever so brightly—do you know this?Do you know where you came from, or how beautiful the light of your soul is? Are you on your path or are you a spectator in your own journey? Are your eyes open or closed? Can you see the light in others, no matter how dark it is at times?

Can you hear the inner sounds of your drum beating? Can you feel your vibration increasing as you serve others with total selflessness? Do you feel the light within you, and that inner ache to connect with Source and who you are?

For you are a spirit fulfilling a human experience, on your path to serve others. In those actions lies the greatest humility of all, the brightness of your soul can never be extinguished but burns ever so brightly as a light for those that are lost in darkness.

Boundaries of the Soul

Dear ones, whenever one hears the word "boundary", think of the vastness of your soul and the journey within

As your mind races towards your inner journey. Reflect on the endless possibilities that lie ahead for you

Feel and breathe in the essence of your inner beauty of spirit and those around you

Be lost in oneself, not in the why or maybes but in the essence of your own stillness, for this where your true self and answers lie.

Rejoice, smile like that of a new born child who gazes with pure soul love into the eyes of its soul parents with an inner karmic knowing of belonging.

It takes but one moment—one thought—to open the inner
gate of your imposed self-boundaries

You are the key to your self—no one else, so open your
door and walk in, as much awaits you. .

The Soul's Movement

You are like pebbles in a stream, moving gently, joined
together by an unseen energy current evolving over time

Before you, dear ones, feel and see through your senses all
the shapes, sizes and colours

Notice that even the largest pebble moves and is in tune
with nature's flow

In that moment of recognition, an inner
stillness envelops you

One's soul transcends back to self, for this is
home and who you are

No words are needed, like pebbles and the flicker of a
candle flame, we are timeless and forever in motion.

Nadia Rise

Nadia is a psychic, a mental and trance medium, an inspirational writer and a spiritual healer.

She brings loving messages, encouragement and inspiration to souls in our world by connecting to loved ones who are in Heaven. Nadia is also fond of giving angelic, oracle and tarot card readings and believes that any prediction is one of the most probable futures and everyone has a free will and power to change many things in their lives.

As an accredited Tibetan Usui Reiki practitioner, during her healing sessions Nadia channels Universal Life Force—the energy of healing, unconditional and purely unselfish love. This energy touches the souls of those who come to her looking for help, enabling them to heal themselves on as many levels as possible and to whatever degree is appropriate for every individual.

Nadia is compassionate, understanding and works with all those who need her help. She practices distant healing for those who live afar. Nadia is an admirer of Aura-Soma and widely uses pomanders for psychic protection and during healing sessions. She loves the breathtaking beauty of nature and appreciates the time when she can stop to smell the roses.

Email: medium.nadia@gmail.com

Let My Soul Soar

Let my soul rise into the sky and fly, fly high
into the sky with no limits

To touch the Sun and see the moon,

To travel to Pluto and Saturn

To see the stars, new planets and realms

With so many spirits and exams

You've never seen or thought enough

Of all the miracles above

Of all the magic in simple things

That make my soul soar and sing

And in the magic of the light

I see the future and the past, of all that
happened to all of us.

Listening to My Soul

In the time of darkness, I keep still and wait for
the voice from inside

That voice will bring me comfort by saying
a message from above

That all that happens has its cause and we cannot change
the unchangeable clause

That we must carry our cross of all the challenges
that we come across

That only in such a way we get to know
wisdom and spiritually grow

Then my soul will smile on me and add

You can carry what you've got—you have the strength

Develop patience, don't abandon hope, revive belief—it
will be such a relief

You know, to be the whole, you need to experience all

All bad and happy times to understand what stands behind

And afterwards you'll get the point and come to us rejoiced

In the Light of the Soul

In the light of the soul I grow

In the light of the soul I get hope

In the light of the soul I shine and believe

In the light of the soul I love and relieve

In the Presence of the Soul

In the presence of the soul you'll be transformed to become a better person in a passionate embrace of love, light, forgiveness and understanding.

Speaking to the Soul

I have a visitor today—an incredibly beautiful soul. The soul shines in the rays of the light and is full of love, compassion and kindness. I smell the soul's presence by an adorable aroma of tea roses and honeysuckle which spread widely in my room. I feel delighted, inspired and at peace.

The soul invites me on a journey and I willingly agree. We magically appear in the divine garden full of beauty and my imagination. The garden is full of flowers in blossom, and beautiful birds chirping in the trees, the sounds of powerful waters is like music to the ears, crystals are shining in the waters of the springs, butterflies are flying in the sky in a circular dance, and the fairies are smiling on us from the bluebells.

The soul looks at me. We have a lot of things to talk about which is not a mundane task. The time has stopped for us. We talk about growth and setbacks, and life in any form. My silent questions answered, and messages received. This all brings such a comfort. And then suddenly I'm back in my room. It is time to say goodbye, till next time. I feel I'm changed and relieved, and all the worries left behind.

I open a window and feel the warmth of the sun. I count my blessings, and give thanks. The journey was beyond comparison. It brought me knowledge and wisdom for which I'm so grateful.

Debra Guillon

Debra is a spiritual healer, a past life regression therapist, a palmist and a teacher. After many years of teaching mainstream children with learning and behavioural difficulties, she is now able to help those in need to understand their own power through spiritual awareness. She works with children and adults to help them grow, by way of expressing themselves, having energy to cope with anxiety and a means to heal.

Website: www.debradawnspiritualservices.com
Email: dguillon@hotmail.com

The Soul

The soul is forever humble. It has no ego to fall back on.

Its glory comes from the clear knowing and
presence of ALL THAT IS.

It is like a star in the sky shining down on all those who
needs its love.

The soul sees no wrong in any situation or any being.
It is a beautiful spark of GOD.

The enlightened being through the ages which guides each
person back to NIRVANA.

The essence of nothingness.

We are all guided by our soul's presence to shine.

Let My Soul Soar

My soul has risen against many obstacles.

Each life, I have been driven to reveal my true self to others
and in each life I have failed to accomplish my soul's
yearning to be completely alive.

Alive in the body I have been given in GRACE, to keep
with me during the journey of life.

I can often no longer go on and on and on to
another and another.

"Why" I sometimes ask, "am I here in this incompetent,
useless body, when I have a soul of love and compassion
and freedom that is everlasting and an enigma to all who
do not come with an open heart?"

My only wish is to be like the Andean condor, to soar and
fly with my beloveds that travel with me through these
journeys called life.

In the Light of My Soul

No wonder I get panic attacks if my soul is going too far,
too fast, to stay close and keep me grounded.

My soul's light must stay close to me at all times,
so that I have the courage to be who I am meant
to be for this lifetime.

Whenever there is a storm brewing, my soul's light guides
me to new adventures. That light is my beacon of courage
to build a strong fortress of love around me. I know that
my path is there to safely tread.

I do not need to ask others for guidance.

Only my own soul can prepare me for life's challenges.

I must stay true to this light as it honours my existence
as a human being. Weaving the magic of life before
me each day of my life. Always.

The Presence of the Soul

Our souls are a unique and wondrous thing.

We each have one.

No living creature is denied a soul. From the lowliest ant to the highest gentry.

We are all unique, I say again.

Yet we are all one, as our souls combine to bring the wondrous love of GOD to Mother Earth.

This earth plain that we say we all love, as we live upon it for sustenance and life.

Your souls are present here and now as you sit in your chair. And, also omnipresent, as it is a light of love and graciousness that binds all living beings together.

Our souls will never die but go on to bring light and love.

For this we are grateful. Our souls are US.

Our presence is our souls.

Listening to My Soul

My Soul, where do you come from?

My heart is yearning for you to come closer to me
as I am longing to linger closer and closer to you,
each day of my life.

Your words are often silent to my ears.

The challenge is unbearable to us driven to be under
GOD'S umbrella of love and compassion.

Where there's a driving force to help others. Let me be of
service to aid and abide by those in need.

To travel on long dusty roads, then up the gravel to the
epitome of love, which is the home where
the heart resides.

Now I am journaling in silence as my soul's
words are revealed.

You can no longer stay silent to me when I ask you to come
closer and speak.

These words you are saying can no longer taunt me as
whispers in the background.

"What was that?" I'd ask.

I listen with my heart open and receptive.

Allowing others to listen as well—if they join me—to the
beauty of GOD, the universal life force of ALL THAT IS.

My Soul's Choice

My soul has a choice to stay or to go, to learn or to ignore,
to be still, to receive, to obey, and to believe.

There are so many choices as we travel down
this path called life.

I came to be aware of my choices by chance.
This is how I learnt of my progress.

To stay faithful to my life path. A path that has brought me
much pleasure, love, compassion for others,
the gift of healing and blessings.

We are not all the same in our choices.

I love to listen to the birds singing, hear beautiful music and
cry, play an instrument or dance.

You may do none of these but your greatest life pleasures
are your choices as your soul knows how to thrive in its
own environment of YOUR body.

I say, "Never say never" because our soul's choice can lead
us to a path that is so open and expansive that our wildest
dreams would never venture there.

Be still to choose and choose with love.

My soul's choice is knowing my journey is an easy
ride of acceptance, truth revealed, intrinsically
magical and forever a lover of life.

Be One with Your Soul

The light of my soul is so near to me, yet so far.

It gathers speed as it draws close to the universal love that some name GOD. God of the heavens.

These GODS can be seen by us in our souls, when we are tired and drained and too weary to search deeper for the true meaning of our lives.

We come together to join with others, yet the others seem so far away, when our soul is not yet open to new ideas.

Ideas to transverse the universe, not just stay grounded in the subtle light of Mother Earth.

Gaia to some. Gaia has so much more to offer when unified with our souls. To bring breath into all that we do as Masters of our own destinies.

You are the light when your soul is shining in JOY from giving and receiving.

The blessings it receives are miraculous and loving.

Be one with your soul. Be its light.

Susan Bate

Susan is a Clairvoyant/Psychic Medium, Reiki Master/
Teacher, Trance Channeller and author. She also
produces spirit drawings.

Susan has worked at Expos and in private homes.
She is a published author and the winner of various
competitions.

MA(Creative Writing), Macquarie Uni), Graduate
Diploma in Counselling (Syd. Uni).

Email: suewrite@ozemail.com.au

The Presence of the Soul

I know you are there, quiet as a whisper, my comfort blanket and the rudder of my ship.

Whoever or whatever I am, I am the search party for new experiences, new challenges, and the filter of grief, disappointment, joy, happiness and finally death.

All of this marked on the Soul's memory as I continue transition after transition on the endless journey that is eternity.

The bridge from this world to another spans the ages, my soul beckoning to come, come, always to come, to gather new experiences and lessons for me to complete.

Where are you, Soul? I know you are there, my unseen observer. If I stand very, very still and quieten my mind for just one moment, I can see where you are in the reflection of me.

The Stillness of My Soul

In the stillness of my Soul I see everything.

In the stillness of my Soul I have a knowing.

In the stillness of my Soul I hear the whisper of the ages.

In the stillness of my Soul I realise my courage.

In the stillness of my Soul I see my own beauty.

In the stillness of my Soul I see me, and I weep.

Beloved, Beloved

Is that the wind I hear or the whisper of my Soul?

How many times have I ignored that whisper?
Far too many, preferring instead to listen to
external prompts and cues.

But the Soul is patient, the Soul will wait for the next
opportunity to whisper in my ear, to prompt my heart,
to teach me what I must know.

And what does it say, my Soul?

Be of joy and at peace

Let your Spirit sing and soar

Let your heart dance and be engaged

Honour your Divinity and bathe in the Light

Don't let your destiny pass you by because you are the
bearer of your Soul's purpose and all else is meaningless.

Let My Soul Soar

Let my Soul soar,

Let my Spirit sing while all else crumbles around me.

Let me fly as I realise my true purpose, my heart
braced for any sorrow to come.

Let my song be sweet, my heart without bitterness as
I fulfil my duty once more.

Let my hands and heart heal and honour the Divinity which
aligns me with the slipstream of life, rising to serve that to
which I am committed. Let it soar and sing and rejoice with
the knowledge of all that I am, bathed in Divine Light
and Love, so that it echoes throughout the Universe and
beyond, bearing one small sliver of light that is me,
to unite with the Great All That Is.

Oh yes, let my Soul Soar as I travel home.

In the Light of the Soul

Whether I stumble or fall then try once more, unaware I am living my life in the Light of the Soul. There can be no other way, it is what it is and so be it. We are joined throughout eternity my Soul and I. But when I stop struggling and am still for just a moment, the Light of my Soul will enter my consciousness and illuminate long forgotten lessons and instil in me a knowingness of who I am and what is expected of me. It was always there that knowledge, waiting for recognition and application, because in the light of the Soul I stand in truth, in the light of the Soul I stand in love and am love, in the light of the Soul I stand as one who unites with All That Is.

Beginning of the
Soul's Journey

Curl yourself within me, we have work to do. Let me feel
your strength, your splendour on this magical voyage,
one that is beyond measure. Come my eternal companion,
my friend, just one more time where we will face the
storms of life, climb the heights of bliss and
ponder the problems of humanity.

We will fly over mountains, swoop into gullies and soar
into clouds, feeling the coolness of the rain on our bodies
and the tingle of the morning rays of the sun. I promise you
the journey will never be dull. It will be testing at times—
drama peppered with moments of tranquillity in
which you will rest and ponder.

You will feel moments of great sorrow and of great joy,
wishing one to pass quickly and the other to linger a little
longer. You will look into the faces of sorrow and weep,
and into the faces of joy and laugh, and into the depths of
hate and be afraid.

Many adventures await us, dear friend, which will be
marked well to reflect your experience and growth, your
every disappointment, your accomplishments and the
lessons you have not yet learned.

We are each other's salvation, intertwined throughout
forever, inextricably linked by Divine Decree, for I am you
and you are me. Let the magic begin.

The Soul Speaks

Tears drop heavily on the arms folded in front of me as I lift my head, slowly and wearily. My heart is heavy and broken and I wonder how much pain a heart can carry. My body is wracked with sorrow. Never again will I look on that face and search it for the meaning that comes from within, or hold that body against me, or race to relate the latest news. The unruly curls that cover your head will no longer enchant me. You are gone from me, perhaps forever.

I turn within to my most intimate holder of secrets, my soul. I need answers and solace from the cruelty of life. I needed an answer to why. Why now? Why, Why, Why?

Why do we need to suffer such pain in order to grow, to suffer such emptiness, to suffer the hollowness from the place where fullness lived? My soul waits patiently for my mind and my heart to settle and for the sobbing to recede before she speaks.

"You forget, dearest one, that growth not only occurs during the most painful of times, but that it also occurs during the blissful times and, yes, during the times of stillness also. You wonder why you must experience the spectrum of life's traumas throughout your life. You already know why but I will remind you.

The joyful times allow you to feel and rejoice in the happiness of another, which enables you to join with their heart in their happiness, and so experience your own. It also contrasts those times when you are less than happy, allowing you to join with the hearts of others who are in pain, to lift and bolster their sorrow, to help heal their pain, whilst understanding and experiencing another version of love that is compassion.

We are a species who are capable of so much love and this opportunity to participate in sorrow allows you to give love, the greatest act in which you can participate. So, in answer to your ultimate question of why this had to happen, dearest friend, it is teaching you to accept and receive love, to allow other souls to offer it to you so that they can experience their own capacity to give and receive love and compassion and thereby grow, and in return you will also grow from this experience.

We are all one, never forget that. Also do not forget that you haven't lost your loved one. They are busy with the next stage of their own journey waiting for your return home."

Kim Hollands

After many years working in mental health, I had the opportunity to work on my spiritual development. On this journey, I have met many amazing people and teachers, from around the world.

My experience and psychic development has come through meditation, developing my intuition, clairvoyance, trance mediumship and healing. I love Tarot and the ability to read intuitively. I have learnt the skill of inner guidance using hypnotherapy.

I joined a spiritualist church where I learnt that the world of Spirit is a wonderful place to be. I am so grateful for all that it has brought into my life, and for all that I hope to be able to share with others as a clairvoyant trance medium.

Email: kimhollands@gmail.com

Blessings for the Soul

All of life is a blessing from God,

The ultimate gift from a powerful source

That allows us to give to our souls

Rejuvenation and renewal

The wisdom and light of God shines down

Through the universe providing all that is
necessary for our souls

To create a world of light beauty and joy

Healing for the Soul

They came for healing and sat in silence

As the hand of the Holy Spirit touched each one

And in a moment of clarity, they were given a blessing.

And each saw the truth that they were free

It's Time to Listen

As the door opens she is standing there.
"I've been waiting for you," she says.

I look at this lady with the dark hair and the dark eyebrows.

She points to the open window into my soul.
"Let's go in there," she says.

I need to talk to you.

We go through a window into a space filled
with bright white light.

She starts to talk to me.

"It's time for you to listen," she says.

The Presence of the Soul

The presence of the soul is in each of us and is the place

Within us that contains each earthly existence

And the knowledge acquired through many lifetimes.
The presence of the soul in each

Of us is the place where the touch of God still exists.

Deep within us lies the knowledge that there is a divine
plan for our soul's journey through this lifetime,

To grow and move forward on its chosen path.

Blessings from the Soul

All of life is a is a blessing from God

The ultimate gift from a powerful source, that allows us to
give our souls rejuvenation and renewal.

The wisdom and light of God shines down through the
universe, providing all that is necessary for our souls

To create a world of light beauty and joy

A Gift for the Soul

The colours of the rainbow shine down from above

A gift from the universe showering us with love

For each soul to interpret and with joy manifest

The magnificent ethereal hand of God at its best

Light up Your Soul

Allow spirit to take you to the top of the mountain,
And show you the love and joy that lies on the other side.

Amongst the stars you will see the golden pathway

That will lead you up to the light, and

Fill your soul with joy

Let Your Soul Soar

As the night air settles around our shoulders

The subtle breadth of Spirit fills our minds

We feel at peace in the darkness, and safe from our fears

As Spirit guides us to breathe deeply

And take in the perfection, before our eyes

As the stars dance in the heavens

Our souls soar up together and become one

In the presence of the eternal

Love of God.

My Soul Listens

I watched in silence while a dense white mist
surrounded my feet,

Then slowly moved up my legs, until it covered
me like a blanket

Then in the stillness the silence spoke to me

And a warm glow filled me with peace

That moment of silence was an opportunity for
my soul to hear

What the universe was trying to tell me, and in that silence

My soul heard the music of God talking. The gentle
rhythms and vibrations

Sending my soul wisdom and comfort

Robin Steel

My life is an endless journey of learning and wonder.
I love helping others. I have survived many terrible things,
yet my inner strength and peace have never died. I have
always experienced the world in many ways, spiritually,
intuitively and empathically. Truth and compassion for
others are both extremely important to me. I love the
water, sitting on a beach or by a lake at sunrise
or sunset and drinking in the energies.

I love the moon, her rays are beautifully healing. Colour and art and music make my soul sing as do smiles and dancing in the rain. I adore being in emerald green forests. Dogs of all kinds are beautiful, panthers and tigers take my breath away. Numbers and science give me immense pleasure. Love brings it all together.

Email: whimisicalworld@gmail.com

Listen to My Soul

We are of love and light

You are here, I am here

We are separate yet we are one, we are now,

Our strength is profound yet we are powerless sometimes

My depth is you, my everything is you,

Feed me with love, notice me daily,

Enjoy me moment by moment, for I am you, I am your life
force, I am your universe

I am your survival,

I teach you, I guide you for you are my treasured existence,

Love is forever, and each transition is joyous and infinite

Yet there are many who do not see,

There are those who sleep through millenniums,

Be joyous we are one with many others and through us the
darkness is decreasing.

The lightness is unfolding, we recognise others and come
together, and each group—no matter how small—is making
a difference. The current negativity is an illusion. Peace and
tranquility are quietly growing before long love and light
will envelop all and become the dominant.

Let My Soul Soar

My soul is quietly watching peacefully noticing each moment. Waiting for my call to notice. Too much time elapses. We have much work to do, much to accomplish. We are all here for a purpose, to bring light and love to all who exist, be they human, animal, microbe, reptile, bird, sea creature, every living thing exists in synergy.

We are bliss, we are love. Every moment, no matter how small, is an opportunity to expand consciousness. We think, we create, and we grow. Our love is limitless, our existence flows through infinity, our strength is increasing, and more and more are listening to their souls. The light is growing brighter and brighter—there is no turning back. We are journeying into a realm of perfect love.

In the Light of My Soul

You are there in the quiet depths of my existence, your beauty and solace ever-present. My protector, the essence that is me, your brilliance is so often dulled by life's imagined business, but never for very long.

Your quiet insistent voice speaks to me until I listen,

Other times I constantly bask in your joy and light, being soothed into total peace.

The Presence of the Soul

We are of Love and Light, you are here, and I am here

We are separate yet we are one, we are now.

Our strength is profound,

Yet feeling powerless sometimes stays around.
My depth is you,

My everything is you. Feed me with love. Notice me daily.

Enjoy me moment by moment. I am your Life Force.

I am your Universe, I am your Survival. I teach you.

I guide you.

For you are my treasured existence.

Love is forever, each transition is joyous and infinite.
There are many who do not see.

We are one with many others. Through us the darkness is
decreasing. There is lightness unfolding.

We recognise there and come together, each group,
no matter how small is making a difference.

The current negativity is just an illusion.
Peace and tranquility are quietly growing,

Before long, love and light will envelop all and
become the dominant.

Power of the Soul

The power within a group is limitless, alone we generate a call to others to unite with us, but to sit in a circle generating energy is essential for our survival.

Many are joining us in the journey, but many more need to awaken. We are here to make change not to sit back and watch the multiple failings that have been occurring for decades.

Too many souls are sleeping, the wisdom of the ancients has become a quiet whisper. In the streets, the deep sadness is tangible, it is time to move, and it is time to regain the equilibrium.

Too many immature beings are promoting the belief that what has come before them is of no use. Their offspring are constantly being taught self-idolatry. Their tales of persecution are rife, yet these creatures despise everything that is not in their world of narcissistic self-absorption. For many they are at what could be called the kindergarten level of development. Their constant aggression, their need to dominate, is no longer to be allowed or tolerated. Their aggression will be negated by our peaceful ways, and our intentions, our power is our eternal gift, and the beauty of our peace needs to envelop these misguided creatures.

Janet Bradbrook

I have served for many years as a Reiki master and a signature cell healer. For me, healing is the most powerful process to balance the body's energy, pertaining to the mental, physical and emotional state.

I am a psychic/clairvoyant medium and Tarot reader, performing spiritual reading and public demonstrations. My spiritual journey has helped me to open my heart and my mind to create opportunities, and remove any obstacles to live in a world filled with love, abundance and joy.

After years of learning and experience, with the support of spirits, I seek the most important journey of soul with creation and life experience. Having understanding of my purpose towards humanity, community and generosity, I become more alive and share my love with others with gratitude.

Email: rosieycjanet@gmail.com

Let My Soul Soar

My spirit motivates my soul, which is active and awaits the search for more light. When I expand the light, my soul speaks to me and connects to Spirit.

My soul awaits being found, while my spiritual search is for deeper meaning and understanding of who I am and what the purpose of my life is.

When my soul and spirit is in harmony, I can create dreams, desire, inspiration and expectations, in which I can gain power through experiences and create my life with dreams, joy and depths of meaning with value.

Listen to My Soul

I listen to my soul's whispers—they always guide
me to my heart.

The best way for me to connect to my soul is through
my inner sense of knowing.

When I acknowledge my soul, I can understand what
the purpose of my life is.

Surrender is to accept the present moment with
unconditional love rather than resist the flow of life.

Life is a gift, having a deep relationship with God that is
the source of all creation.

When I open my heart I allow myself to be in harmony
with everything in creation.

The Higher Self is always with me as my companion
and guides me to the path of my soul with self-realisation of
unconditional love, so I can create a life I live
without limitations.

In the Light of the Soul

My soul is always there to guide me. With every step towards fulfilling my destiny, it creates opportunities. My soul dreams with the life I love to live.

In the heart of silence, I can sense more of the essence of my life. It encourages me so deeply to connect with the source of love, joy, inspiration and abundance.

I surrender all my negatives, and the past, and move forward without fear or hesitation, so that I can change to manifest the universe and achieve what I desire.

Stand in the Presence of the Soul

The soul is pure energy it exists in the heart of our soul.
I am always confused at the beginning. What is soul about?

The soul is what we sense—we can sense someone like
Spirit, and it is the essence of life
Through our soul and consciousness we can sense and feel
the depth of feelings deep within.
When we are within the presence of the soul, we can gain
power and look for more love and freedom.

When we have freedom to love, we open our hearts and
have a clear mind to perceive a whole new way in the
world to experience what we have never known before.
When we meditate, our souls speak to us in the stillness
and communicate to us information and
guidance we need to know.
The most common way to experience its presence
is to connect to nature.
We can sense the beauty that exists within all life. It can be
simply watching a sunset or walking or sitting in nature.

Nature is the most inspirational gift—it assists us to stay in
the present moment, the magnificent beauty and creation
of nature is life's greatest gift. We realise God is with us,
hand in hand.

When our soul experiences sorrow and loss, that helps
us to feel deeper compassion and love, so it is with
gentleness that we can find joy again.

The presence of our soul embraces the love that is beyond
everything we can imagine and our soul is with us always.

Shauna O'Donnell

I am a spiritual and energetic healer, a Reiki master, an angel intuitive, a psychic medium, an intuitive reader, a serenity vibration healer, an NLP practitioner, a time line therapy® practitioner.

I have a passion for crystals and an innate desire to help others. I have an interest in palmistry and hypnotherapy among other things. I see every day as an opportunity to learn something new. I feel most at peace out in nature.

Email address: shauna.odonnell1@gmail.com

In the Light of the Soul

Light beams into the hearts of all encouraging love to spread. Peace and calm envelopes us, making individuals aware of the existence of others, many others, urging us to come together as one, once more.

In the Presence of the Soul

Daylight breaks the darkness, warming and expanding the heart, raising our soul's consciousness. Peace and tranquillity exude beyond the limits of the physical world. One by one, souls connect, encapsulating the world and expanding out in the universe.

The connection of the souls elevates the vibration of the earthly world, raising awareness in individuals to take better care of their world and love their fellow man.

Listen to My Soul

As I sit in silence, I am aware of a voice inside me, a voice
that emanates feelings of love, trust and faith.

The sense of peace is intoxicating and exhilarating.
Feelings I want to feel every second of the day.
Sensations I want to guide me. I become aware that all
I have learned on this plane is irrelevant and I need only
follow the loving voice inside!

Let My Soul Soar

Looking down on my physical body from high above,
feelings of gratitude wash over my soul.
Though the path I have walked so far has not been easy,
I am grateful for the lessons learnt.

Moving forward on my journey will be easier now,
knowing I have let go and forgiven myself and others,
lightening the load.

Judgement and expectation is a weight that will no longer
drag my spirit down—it has no place in my world.

CPSIA information can be obtained
at www.ICGtesting.com
Printed in the USA
BVOW10s1735250817
5879BVAU00005B/6/P